THE
White Horse

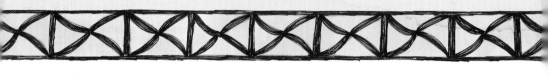

When old Papa got sick,
he had Mum's and Dad's bed.
Mum and Dad slept on the floor
with us children.

In the morning, all the little kids
got into bed with Papa.
He told us stories about the old days
and about his dreams.
We liked the white-horse dreams best.

"He came again last night," said Papa,
"so close, I nearly caught him."

"Where was he?" we asked.

"Under the mango trees," said Papa.
"Big, he was, and as white as moonlight.
There was no wind,
but his mane and tail waved in
the air like the surf on the reef.
His eyes were like black coral.
Cunning old eyes,
they were."

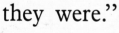

"What'd he do?" we asked.

"Nothing much," said Papa.
"He trotted up to this house –
trot, trot, right up to my bed.
Then he tossed his head
and went away.

"I tried to follow him.
In my dream,
I ran through the village, after him.
I called him, but he wouldn't wait for me."

"What would happen if you caught him?"
we asked.

"I'd ride him, of course," Papa replied.
"With a horse like that,
I could ride clear across the sea
to the morning sun.

"We'd race through the clouds, he and I.
We'd gallop down the sides of rainbows.
Have you ever wanted
to ride down a rainbow?"

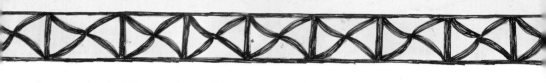

We laughed,
thinking about old Papa doing that.
"You'd fall off," we said.

Papa closed his eyes.
"That's enough dream for one day.
Time for cheeky kids to go to school."

Dad was listening.
"Have you kids been annoying Papa?"

Old Papa laughed.
"They're all right," he said.
"They're good kids."

16

18

Soon after that, old Papa got sick again and went into hospital.

In the middle of the night he died.

The next morning,
his sons brought him back.
They walked from the hospital,
through the pineapple and taro gardens,
home to the village.

Everyone else followed, singing and crying.

Old Papa's coffin was filled
with leaves and frangipani flowers.
It was put on a mat
in the middle of the house.
We sat beside it with Mum and Dad.

The body looked like Papa,
but Papa wasn't in it.

I asked Dad, "Where's Papa gone?"

Dad held my hand.

"Papa caught the white horse," he said.